Anthony Umelo

The Midnight Caller

J•A•W•S

Text illustrations by Avril Turner
Cover illustration by Paul Harrison

Series Editor: Karen Morrison

Heinemann

Heinemann Educational Publishers
A division of Heinemann Publishers (Oxford) Ltd
Halley Court, Jordan Hill, Oxford OX2 8EJ

Heinemann Educational Books (Nigeria) Ltd
PMB 5205, Ibadan
Heinemann Educational Boleswa
PO Box 10103, Village Post Office, Gaborone, Botswana

FLORENCE PRAGUE PARIS MADRID
ATHENS MELBOURNE JOHANNESBURG
AUCKLAND SINGAPORE TOKYO
CHICAGO SAO PAULO

British Library Cataloguing in Publication Data
A catalogue record for this book is available
from the British Library

ISBN 0 435 89179 0

Glossary
Difficult words are listed alphabetically on page 29

Edited by Christine King
Designed by The Point
Printed and bound in Great Britain

96 97 98 99 10 9 8 7 6 5 4 3 2 1

John Gana woke up suddenly, wondering where he was. Then he remembered. Back at home in bed, of course!

He couldn't remember going to bed. He had fallen asleep in the taxi on the way home from the airport. He and his parents had flown in late at night from London, where they had been on holiday.

John looked at the clock. It was late. But it was Sunday, so he didn't have to go to school.

John got up. As he washed and dressed, he wished it wasn't Sunday. He wanted to go to school and tell his friends all about his exciting trip. He had been away for a month, and he had seen all sorts of interesting things.

He joined his parents in the living room. They were still eating breakfast.

'Good morning,' John said.

'Hello there,' his father said. 'Did you sleep well?'

'Oh yes!' John replied. 'I don't think I even had any dreams.'

His mother said, 'We knew you were tired. That's why we let you sleep for so long.'

John ate his breakfast while his father read the newspaper. When John finished he said to his father, 'Are you going to work on the car this morning?'

'Yes, I am,' said his father. 'Would you like to help?'

Before they went on holiday, Mr Gana had put his car in the garage. He had taken off the wheels and removed the battery so that no one could steal the car.

John was happy to help. He loved cars. He played with toy cars and collected pictures of different types of car.

He and his father went to the garage.

Mr Gana unlocked the heavy garage door. The car was covered in dust.

'It is very dirty,' he said. 'We will wash it when we have finished.' This was good news for John. If they washed the car he could play with the soapy water.

Mr Gana sent John to fetch the wheels while he connected the battery. He had hidden the wheels in a shed round the side of the house.

As John walked to the shed, he thought
about his holiday in London. He tried to
decide which stories he would tell his friends
first.

Suddenly he felt funny. He was sure that
someone was watching him. He looked
around, but he saw nobody. Then he saw a
movement behind the wall, next to the
mango tree.

The mango tree moved a little more and John saw a man looking over the wall. The man was very tall and he looked very angry. John stood still and stared at him.

Suddenly, the man saw John standing there. He gave John a fierce look that scared him. But before John could move, or call his father, the man walked away very quickly.

Who was the man? And why had he looked at John like that?

John ran back and told his father about the man. Mr Gana went round to the tree and looked over the wall. He looked up and down the street, but there was no sign of any man.

'Are you sure you saw somebody?' Mr Gana asked John.

'Yes, I really did.' John knew he hadn't imagined the man, and his fierce look.

'Well, there's nobody here now,' said his father. 'Let's go and get the wheels.'

John and his father took a long time to put
the wheels back on the car. It was almost
lunch time before Mr Gana drove the car out
of the garage.

After lunch, he and John washed the car.
John liked doing this. He worked so hard that
he forgot about the strange man and his
fierce look.

In bed that night, John couldn't sleep. He thought about his holiday again and the stories he would tell at school the next day.

Suddenly, he heard a strange noise outside. He ran over to the window and looked out. Something was moving on the wall by the mango tree.

It was an arm, gripping the wall. The arm was followed by a leg. Next a head appeared. It was the man John had seen earlier!

John was terrified. He was unable to move. He saw the man jump into the garden and land near the mango tree. He was looking at the house.

Was he a thief? Was he going to come into the house?

John did not realise he had screamed. The next moment his mother and father rushed into his room.

'What's the matter, John?' they asked. 'Have you had a nightmare?'

'No,' said John. He was shaking. 'I saw that man again. He climbed over the wall and he was looking at our house.'

Mr Gana opened the window and looked outside, but the man had already gone.

'It was a nightmare,' he said. 'Go back to sleep now, John. You have school tomorrow.'

John went back to bed, but for a long time he was too afraid to sleep.

In the morning John could hardly keep his eyes open. He was too tired to be excited about seeing his friends.

His mother told him not to worry about his nightmare.

'It was not a dream!' he shouted. 'The man was real.'

His parents were very worried. They went out to the mango tree and looked on the ground. Sure enough, there were footprints under the tree. There were also marks on the wall. Mr Gana decided to call the police.

John went to school and told his friends all about London. He did not tell them about the man in case they did not believe him.

He arrived home that afternoon just as a policeman was knocking at the door.

'Hello,' said the policeman. He had a big gun. 'You must be John. I am Sergeant Moloi. I have come to see your father.'

Mr Gana opened the door and shook hands with Sergeant Moloi.

The sergeant asked John to show him where the man had been. Mr Gana went with them to the mango tree.

The policeman could see clearly where the man had jumped down. The footprints were very big and deep.

'John was right, Mr Gana,' said Sergeant Moloi with a frown. 'There really was a man in your garden!'

Mr Gana was shocked and worried. 'Do you think the man will come back?' he asked Sergeant Moloi.

'We don't know,' said the sergeant, 'but it's best to make sure.'

'How can we do that?' asked Mr Gana.

'We can set a trap,' said the policeman. 'I will come back here later, with some of my assistants. Then if the man comes, we will be ready!'

The sergeant smiled at John. 'Don't worry,' he said. 'We will catch him.'

In the evening the police came to the Ganas' house. They moved quietly so they would not attract any attention.

They decided to keep watch from the lounge. They took it in turns to look through the window.

John was too excited to sleep, so his parents let him stay up. John kept watch from the window of his own room, while his parents remained downstairs with the police.

At midnight John saw the arm coming over the wall again, followed by the leg. He hurried downstairs and whispered to Sergeant Moloi, 'He's come!'

'Where?' the sergeant asked quietly.

'There, by the mango tree,' John replied.

'Oh yes. I can see him now,' said the policeman.

The man jumped down from the wall. First he stood looking at the house. Then he moved slowly and silently like a cat towards the garage. In his right hand he carried a large pair of cutters.

'He is going to steal our car,' John said. 'You have to stop him.'

'Not yet,' said Sergeant Moloi. 'Let's wait and see what he does.'

At the garage door, the man quickly cut through the lock with his tool. He stood quite still and looked around, then he carefully pushed the garage door open.

Sergeant Moloi waited until the man disappeared into the garage. Then he said, 'Let's go. But do nothing until he comes out. We'll be waiting for him.'

The police left silently through the back door. John and his father followed them.

The police waited outside the garage, not making a sound. John and his father waited too.

They could all hear the man moving around inside. It sounded as if he was searching for something. John wondered what it could be.

After a short time they heard the man mutter, 'Ah, got it!'

The man stepped out of the door. He was carrying a plastic bag in one hand, the cutters in the other. The police rushed to grab him.

They caught the man by surprise, and managed to get the large tool away from him. But the man was big and strong, and he put up a fight. He kicked and punched and swore. Sergeant Moloi received a punch on the nose that made his eyes water.

As the man struggled with the police, the bag fell on the ground and burst open. Suddenly there was money everywhere!

Finally the struggle was over. The police managed to put handcuffs on the man's wrists. Sergeant Moloi and two of his assistants dragged him round to the back door. The other two stayed at the garage to pick up the money. John and his father followed the man.

Sergeant Moloi glared at the man in the light.

'Phew!' he said. 'It looks like we've caught Henry Toba.'

John knew who Henry Toba was. He had read about the bank robbery before he left for London. The robbers had stolen thousands of dollars. They had also injured a bank clerk and a security guard.

The police had suspected Toba, but they had not arrested him because they could not find the money.

Henry Toba hid the money from the robbery in the Ganas' garage. But the family had come back from holiday before he could remove it, and he had to sneak in to get it. John had spoiled Toba's plans by spotting him at the mango tree.

Toba looked at John. His eyes were very angry. John was glad that he was handcuffed.

As the police took Toba away, Sergeant
Moloi spoke to John.

'Well done,' he said. 'There'll probably be a
reward for this. And don't worry about Toba.
He will be going to jail for a long time.'

Toba said nothing at all. He just gave John
a horrible look. John was glad to see him go.

When the police had all left, Mr Gana said, 'You were right all along, John, and you deserve that reward.'

But John was yawning so hard that he couldn't reply.

His mother said, 'Reward or no reward, John, it's two o'clock in the morning and you're going to bed.'

John smiled as he went upstairs. He was just glad that the midnight caller would not be calling on them any more!

Questions

1 Where had John been on holiday?

2 Why had John's father taken the wheels off his car?

3 Where did John first see the man?

4 Why did his father and mother not believe he had seen a man?

5 What did the police do to catch the man?

6 Why did the man want to get into Mr Gana's garage?

7 Why do you think the man fought and kicked when the police tried to catch him?

8 Who was the man?

Activities

1 Find some words in the story that describe the man. Try to add some more words of your own to the list.

2 Think about a holiday that you have had. Draw a picture of what you did and where you went.

3 John is going to tell his friends all about the man in the garden. Pretend you are John and tell the story as if it happened to you.

Glossary

airport (page 1) the place where aeroplanes take off and land

cutters (page 19) a strong tool that can cut through metal

fierce (page 7) angry and nasty

glared (page 23) looked at angrily

handcuffs (page 23) strong metal rings joined by a short chain which the police use to keep prisoners' hands tied at the wrist

imagined (page 8) thought something was real when it was not

nightmare (page 12) a very frightening dream

reward (page 26) payment for doing a good deed

suspected (page 24) believed to be a criminal

terrified (page 11) very, very frightened

The Junior African Writers Series is designed to provide interesting and varied African stories both for pleasure and for study. There are five graded levels in the series.

Level 2 is suited to readers who have been studying English for four to five years. The content and language have been carefully controlled to increase fluency in reading.

Content The plots are simple and the number of characters is kept to a minimum. The information is presented in small manageable amounts and the illustrations reinforce the text.

Language Reading is a learning experience and, although the choice of new words is carefully controlled, new words that are important to the story are also introduced. These are contextualised and explained in the glossary. They also appear in other stories at Level 2.

Glossary Difficult words which learners may not know have been listed alphabetically at the back of the book. The definitions refer to the way a word is used in the story, and the page reference is for the word's first use.

Questions and **Activities** The questions give useful comprehension practice and ensure that the reader has followed and understood the story. The activities develop themes and ideas introduced and can be done as pairwork or groupwork in class, or as homework.

JAWS Starters
In addition to the five levels of JAWS titles, there are three levels of JAWS Starters. These are full-colour picture books designed to lead in to the first level of JAWS.